My Mother's
KEEPER

Transforming Life Challenges Into Opportunities of Self-Discovery

Sheila D. Williams, Ph.D.

Table of Contents

Dedication ix

Forward xi

Chapter 1:   I Think I Can.... 15

Chapter 2:   Silence.... 19

Chapter 3:   The Empty Nest 21

Chapter 4:   Responsibility... 25

Chapter 5:   Just Be.... 31

Chapter 6:   Role Reversal.... 35

Chapter 7:   The Eye Of The Sparrow.... 39

Chapter 8:   I'm Still Here... 43

Chapter 9:   What Mom Took.... 47

Chapter 10: Why Me? 51

Chapter 11: The Forgotten Promise.... 55

Chapter 12: Peace Be Still.... 63

Chapter 13: Don't Be Disillusioned... 67

Chapter 14: It Is Well.... 73

My Mother's
KEEPER

Proverbs 22:6

Train up a child in the way he should go: and when he is old, he will not depart from it.

Dedication

This book is dedicated to the woman who inspired me to be me. She was a woman of few words, but who spoke profoundly through her actions. Through her endeavors to live as a godly woman, and the love she shared for her husband and for her children, she found happiness. She was a woman of God, a virtuous woman: a woman undefiled and dedicated to the well-being of her family. She was soft-spoken, slow to speak, methodical, mysterious, intriguing and elegant in every way in which she carried herself. She was a humble and devoted wife, mother, friend and Christian. She was a homemaker, a sister, an aunt and a daughter. She was a phenomenal woman. She was my best-friend. She was my mother.

Mattie Williams, this book is dedicated to you. For without you as my mother and my best friend, I would not, could not, be the woman I am today. I'm forever indebted to you for making me the woman I am now and for who I will become. I exist because of you.

I loved you then, I love you now, and I'll forever love you.

Sheila

Forward

*F*or every woman that is a mother, has lost her mother or is currently caring for their aging mother, I write this book for you. It is with this compilation of memories and experiences I write this book, as a means to express the love one woman can share for another. The bond a mother shares with her daughter is like no other love that can be shared. To not only share the same blood, but to have experienced unselfish love and a nurturing upbringing, one can only give respect and admiration for the love that only a mother and daughter could share. It is that same love that leads to a fulfilling and well-balanced adulthood. Having been blessed to be born to a phenomenal woman, I have no choice but to write this book, as I know I am not alone.

As you read this, my only request is that you share it with your daughters, your stepdaughters, your goddaughters and your mothers. Motherhood, and in my opinion "daughterhood", is a gift from God. I ask that you share this book with others, as some of my experiences could in fact be yours now or maybe yours in the years to come.

My mother, Mattie Williams, was the epitome of what a woman, a mother, should be. She taught me the meaning of hard work, humility, commitment and perseverance. She was a beautiful being inside and out, an angel given to us for only a short period of time. A delicate flower that blossomed in season, she graciously wilted until her time was no more. I am blessed to be the seed of her existence.

Proverbs 31:10-31, KJV

Who can find a virtuous woman? for her price is

far above rubies.

The heart of her husband doth safely trust in her,

so that he shall have no need of spoil.

She will do him good and not evil all the days of

her life.

She seeketh wool, and flax, and worketh willingly

with her hands.

She is like the merchants' ships; she bringeth her

food from afar.

She riseth also while it is yet night, and giveth
meat to her household, and a portion to her
maidens.

She considereth a field, and buyeth it: with the
fruit of her hands she planteth a vineyard.

She girdeth her loins with strength, and strength-
eneth her arms.

She perceiveth that her merchandise is good: her
candle goeth not out by night.

She layeth her hands to the spindle, and her
hands hold the distaff.

She stretcheth out her hand to the poor; yea, she
reacheth forth her hands to the needy.

She is not afraid of the snow for her household:
for all her household are clothed with scarlet.

She maketh herself coverings of tapestry; her
clothing is silk and purple.

Her husband is known in the gates, when he sit-
teth among the elders of the land.

She maketh fine linen, and selleth it; and deliv-
ereth girdles unto the merchant.

Strength and honour are her clothing; and she
shall rejoice in time to come.

She openeth her mouth with wisdom; and in her
tongue is the law of kindness.

She looketh well to the ways of her household,
and eateth not the bread of idleness.

Her children arise up, and call her blessed; her
husband also, and he praiseth her.

Many daughters have done virtuously, but thou
excellest them all.

Favour is deceitful, and beauty is vain: but a
woman that feareth the LORD, she shall be
praised.

Give her of the fruit of her hands; and let her
own works praise her in the gates.

Chapter 1

I Think I Can....

*Y*ou want me to do what? This was what I was thinking at five years old, having never spent a day or night away from my family, and it was the first day of kindergarten for me. *You want me to get out of the car and walk into this building, with hundreds of kids and teachers; but let's face it, you call them teachers but to me they were strangers, and you want me to stay here all day, seven hours? You can't be serious!* So, the tears came. Not knowing how to feel, what to think, how to act or what to say, she talked to me, encouraged me, motivated me and told me all about the "fun" I'd have and all the new friends I'd meet, now that I'm in this new thing they called kindergarten.

To me, you could have taken kindergarten and left it where you found it. I could really have cared less about kindergarten and all the people, things and specifics that come with it. For weeks, Mom tried her best to flip and twist and spin kindergarten, and this whole thing they call "school", to a place that would be interesting and intriguing for me. It didn't work. She cooked my favorite foods, told me all about how all of the kids in the neighborhood would be there with me, how she'd only be a call away and how once I started going, I'd "love" it. *Oh, so that's what you say, but for me there was nothing worse that could have been done to me. Why would I want to leave the comforts of my own home? Why would I want to leave the place, people and surroundings that I know? Why would I want to be around strangers? Better yet, why would you even want me to be around strangers? I thought you told me not to even talk to strangers; now you expect me to hang out with these people? Something's not right with this picture.* For the life of me, in my five-year-old mind, I just couldn't understand.

Little did I know Mom had a master plan for all of the things I couldn't understand. Because she took the time to empathize with why and how her five-year-old daughter felt about this whole "school" thing, she came up with a rhyme and a new, little song-and-dance game. To keep my mind off of "school" and kindergarten and kids, and teachers and STRANGERS, she would start to sing the lyrics to one of the books she would read to me at bedtime. Who knew Mommy had a beautiful voice that she was now singing to me? *Wow, she's even cooler than I thought she was.* The song had a beat, had a vibe, and had a rhythm that caught my attention.

"I think I can. I think I can. I think I can. I know I can."

–Little Engine That Could

There she was: singing and dancing, and pointing and rocking, and throwing her hair back and to the side. She took this opportunity to let me know that just like the Little Engine That Could, I could too. She encouraged me to repeat, "I think I can" until I finally ended with "I know I can". I recited that every day: actually, I sang it every day she drove me to school. I sang it in the car; I sang it in the shower; and I sang it silently to myself. At this point, yes five years old, I realized that Mom was not only Mom, she was my friend; she was cool. We talked, we laughed, and she took the fear out of the unknown. Mom had "swag", even before swag was swag. How did she know? Is this what they call maternal instinct? Her reassurance, her thoughtful way of keeping it real and keeping me focused on believing in myself; it was just enough, exactly enough, for me to overcome my anxiety with this thing called school.

Ephesians 6:2, KJV

Honour thy father and mother;

(which is the first commandment with promise)

No longer did I despise and dread getting in that car and

going to school; I now looked
forward to it. I had friends, and
I made good grades. It wasn't
initially that way for me; it was
a long road, but by third grade
I was reading two to three
grade levels ahead of the other

kids in my class. Although I was still shy, school was fun; the
thought of learning intrigued me. There it was, the seed was
planted; I had been inspired by education and looked forward
to whatever it had to bring.

*My Mother was the most beautiful woman I ever
saw. All I am I owe to my Mother. I attribute all
my success in life to the moral, intellectual and
physical education I received from her.*

George Washington

Chapter 2

Silence...

*M*om knew what she was doing; she had the natural ability to get things done and to bridge the gap without ever saying much at all. In fact, Mom was shy: other than her family, her husband and three kids, she didn't talk much. A woman of few words, so much so at times she would sit and simply look. Yes, give you "the look". She had several looks: the look of a stare, which meant she knew you had done something you weren't supposed to do; the look of innocence, which meant "there's so much more I want to share with you, my child, but you're just too young to understand"; The look of happiness, which meant "I'm not rich, I'm not famous, but I'm a wife, a mother, a child of God and that's all I need." There was the look of frustration; at times she was frustrated that she wasn't outspoken and educated at the level she wanted to be. Then there was the look of mystery; the look that meant, "There's so much more to me than you will ever know."

Mom's silence started long before she was a wife or a mother. She was shy and didn't engage or embrace meeting new people or having conversations with people she didn't know well. She was quiet; even at times she was quiet at home with her own family. As a young child, I didn't understand her silence, but as I got older, I matured and I came to know there was meaning behind the quietness. After bonding with Mom and realizing she was actually pretty cool, I began to see her outside of being just "Mom". I realized that her looks, her stares, her silence all had meaning.

Motherhood is a great honor and privilege, yet it is also synonymous with servanthood. Every day women are called upon to selflessly meet the needs of their families. Whether they are awake at night nursing a baby, spending their time and money on less-than-grateful teenagers, or preparing meals, moms continuously put others before themselves.

Charles Stanley

Chapter 3

The Empty Nest

When I looked at Mom, it was as if I was looking in the mirror: she staring at me and me staring at her. I began to think, and then eventually asked, "What are you thinking about?" Most often, the answer would be "Nothing, I'm just tired". She'd flip the conversation and would then ask me, "How was your day?" or "How are you feeling?" How'd she do that? Better yet, *why* did she do that? Not allowing it to happen any longer, I needed her to know I saw her, I heard her and I had been observing her. She was attentive to every need I had, but in doing so, she put herself last. I was young, but I was old enough to know she needed a friend: someone who accepted her as just being her; knowing she was not perfect; knowing she held secrets; knowing she was still so innocent, and at times more innocent and naïve than I was myself.

I was about nine years old when my only sister left home for college, and a year later my only brother left for the military. At ten years old, I became, in essence, an only child. At ten years old, I became best friends with my mother (and my father). Because there wasn't anyone home but Mom and I, we did everything together. We shopped, we talked, we laughed, we sang, we took walks, she cried, I cried; we existed in knowing we were more alike than we were different. I saw myself in her and she saw herself in me. On Sundays, we dressed alike for church. She showed me how to balance a checkbook, how to manage money and pay bills. We cooked together, prepared meals for my dad (who worked over eighty hours a week), and did laundry. She taught me how to clean the house, how to make my bed (the right way), how to wash and care for my own hair, how to iron my clothes, how to apply makeup, and the list goes on. Mom was missing her two oldest children; and with her husband, my dad, being the sole breadwinner, Mom was lonely. She was experiencing the "empty nest" syndrome, but the only problem was the nest wasn't empty; I was still there and I was only ten years old.

One day, Mom and I were in the kitchen when she turned to me and said, "You're not a baby anymore, so I won't treat you like one." I didn't really know what she meant, but what I did know was that my life, the way I once knew it, was over. The silence she once had was still there, but now I realized that there was a deeper meaning to her silence. Mom had experienced things she had held onto for her entire life. She loved her family, but she was just like any other woman; she had experienced hurt, pain and sadness at various stages in her life. She sat me down one day and said to me, "They were mean to me." When I asked her whom she was referring to, she never really answered. I just knew that she meant that as a child she experienced things she didn't really want to elaborate on, and she never did. She would let me fill in the gaps. She told me that she was always shy, never really talked much and around elementary school age, approximately ten years old, she completely stopped talking for an extended amount of time. At ten years old, I couldn't really understand why she would just *stop talking*, other than thinking something really bad must have happened to her.

1 Corinthians 10:13, KJV

There hath no temptation taken you but such as is common to man: but God is faithful, who will not suffer you to be tempted above that ye are able; but will with the temptation also make a way to escape, that ye may be able to bear it.

My heart broke for what she may have experienced as a child. My heart broke because I empathized with her and how she must have felt. I wanted to understand and know what had occurred: I wanted to right whatever wrong had been done to her. I wanted to make them hurt as they made her hurt. I wanted to help my mother, but I didn't know how. After speaking with my aunts and uncles, they told me that Mom had always been quiet; but around nine or ten years old, they told me that my mother stopped talking altogether until several years later she began to speak, but only a few words with a select group of family and close friends. It was not ironic, but it was meant that at this very same age, ten years old, she would confide in me the things that caused her to be the woman she was. Little did I know my mom's experiences would later shape my entire existence. Her experiences, our conversations and the relationship I had with my mom would lead me to later pursue and obtain a master's degree in mental health counseling and an extensive career in psychology. I needed to understand her silence, why she often chose to not have friends or to socialize with others. I wanted to understand her personality and the way in which she perceived and communicated with others. I needed to know about the mental health and the psychological makeup of my mother in order to better know and understand myself.

Chapter 4

Responsibility...

*I*t was at this point in my young life, yes ten years old, that I was given some pretty serious responsibilities. I did my own laundry and cooked most of my own meals, dressed myself, cleaned the house and ironed my own clothes: it was as if I grew up overnight. Mom knew I could handle it; in fact, I embraced it. Although I was the youngest, I was the one who if you gave me a task "too large", I'd show you how to get it done and get it done effortlessly. She knew she was preparing me for what was to come. When she said she wasn't going to treat me like a baby, she meant it. At times she would not feel well, so she left the household responsibilities to me. She suffered from major migraines and what would later be diagnosed as clinical depression. She often spent hours in bed, asleep or watching television. I'd come in her bedroom to check on her, to bring her water and to rub her hair. Most often, she wouldn't say much, but at times, we would engage in conversations about life. She taught me how to persevere, how to ignore the uncomfortable and to get things done, in spite of being tired, being in pain or even when I may not understand.

Mom kept a lot of her past pain bottled up inside. To this day, I still don't know what really happened to her. She held on to all the hurt and all the past, no matter how bad it was. She kept it all to herself. She confided in me that life for her was not always good, which was something that was obvious by the way in which she hid most of her feelings. She was born in 1937, second generation separated from slavery; she was born the ninth of ten children. She told stories of her picking cotton and working in the fields. Her family lived on a farm in rural Alabama. Times were hard, and the country had just experienced the Great Depression: no television, no video games, no Internet, no malls, no amusement parks; just work life on the farm and family chores. She said that she was always "different" and that no one really understood her, as she was not like the other children. She said that because she wouldn't talk, her parents and older siblings would beat her in order to make her talk. This was probably all they knew how to do, as there was no therapy or mental health counseling back then. In spite of the beatings, she said she was loved and she loved her family, but she said she remained quiet. I often wondered and asked, "Mom, who hurt you?" She never answered. I held on to resentment for many years for what had obviously happened to my mother. Someone had done her wrong, in what way I didn't know. I didn't know whom, I didn't know how and I didn't know when, but her depression told it all.

"Every man has his secret sorrows which the world knows not; and often times we call a man cold when he is only sad."

Henry Wadsworth Longfellow

The responsibility of my daily chores, school, cleaning the house and caring for myself was a little challenging for me, especially at the age of ten years old. What became a true challenge was the responsibility of caring for my mother. She didn't need me to physically care for her at this point, but she needed emotional reassurance that she would be "okay" with just being Mom. No matter what she had gone through, what happened to her and caused her to be so quiet, she wanted to be unconditionally loved, accepted and appreciated. Although she had that from my father, I often felt that my mother wanted to accomplish educational, and perhaps professional, goals that she never pursued because she had a family. It's the story of most women, most wives and most mothers: we sacrifice ourselves in order to be there and care for our children, our families. Mom was no exception.

I realized that now that my siblings were grown and had left home, Mom was letting go: she was tired. Even though I was only ten years old, her depression would not allow her to carry on the "secret" any longer. She had successfully held it together for the eighteen years she raised my sister and brother. Mom never felt comfortable enough to tell her own story, so here I am to tell her story for her.

"I think that the best thing we can do for our children is to allow them to do things for themselves, allow them to be strong, allow them to experience life on their own terms, allow them to take the subway... let them be better people, let them believe more in themselves."

C. JoyBell C.

C. Joybell C is author of poetry and literature books that are mysterious, philosophical and esoteric. She has been quoted to believe that her words are quoted by movers and shakers of this age (people she often refers to as being "much bigger" than herself). She is believed to be a genuine source of inspiration, transformation and discovery for many the world over.

Chapter 5...

Just be...

Mom gave me the responsibility of a lifetime; the responsibility of a daughter caring for her mother. So, at ten years old, my life began. Excelling in school and making a commitment to myself, and to my mother (and my father), I'd do well in school, graduate high school and go on to complete advanced degrees: it was a given. Only spoken of once or twice, and understood that failure would not be an option for me, I began to pour myself into school and my studies, and I loved it. Extracurricular activities were my way of interacting with children my own age; again, I was the only child at home, essentially at times feeling as if I was in fact *the only child*. Most days after school, Mom and I spent a lot of time just "being": we'd sit for hours on end, never saying a word. My presence seemed to comfort her; she would often apologize for not being as smart or outgoing as some of the other women who were her age. Mom apologized for not having a college education; she apologized for not singing in the church choir; she apologized for not having a career and not being like some of the other women who had full-time jobs and lives outside of their families. Mom said she felt that my sister, who was nine and a half years older than me, had wished she had another mother. I'm not sure if she ever told Mom that, but for some reason, Mom had come to that conclusion. As a result, she seemed to internalize her insecurities even more. She said my sister resented her because she was not like other mothers; so she apologized to me for not being able to speak eloquently as other sisters in the church. She often questioned if I felt the same as my sister and would ask if I was happy with her as my mother.

Mom was overly concerned about falling short compared to other mothers, but with me, she had to never worry about that. She needed to not concern herself with trying to impress me or being like any other woman. I could have cared less if she had a degree, had a career, sang in the church choir, or if she held an executive office. I didn't even care if she talked: I was happy with her silence, her sense of humor, her cooking and her quirky ways. I loved her and accepted her just the way she was, and I told her that every chance I got. She need not be anyone other than herself. She was my mother and my best friend, and was beautiful just the way she was. She loved me for being me, being her daughter. She loved me unconditionally, and I loved her just the same. I let her know that all she had to do was just be. She was perfect just being herself, Mattie Williams, imperfect and innocent as she was; that was enough for me.

Chapter 6

Role Reversal...

As my relationship with my mom blossomed, I began to take on more of a caregiver role for her. I whipped through middle school, then on to high school. By the time I was fourteen years old, I was starting my first job, stocking shelves and hanging clothes at K-Mart. Mom's health started to deteriorate, but none of the doctors could explain what was going on with her. There was no diagnosis, other than depression, migraines and high blood pressure. I most often accompanied Mom to her doctors' appointments, because Dad was working. From doctor to doctor we went, in search of an explanation for her constant body aches, fatigue and overall lack of inconsistency in overall health. No one could explain why some days she would feel as if she couldn't walk: her legs hurt; her hands ached, so much so she would often sleep to escape the pain.

For the life of us, we needed to know what was wrong with Mom, but no one seemed to know. Perhaps it was because we didn't have medical insurance, but I didn't make this correlation until I was much older. You see, Mom graduated high school and married the love of her life, my father, shortly thereafter. Dad was a very traditional man, very old-fashioned in his upbringing and the way in which he treated and loved my mom. He was the sole breadwinner in our home; he didn't allow my mom to work. He opened Mom's doors, brought her flowers, held her hand and kissed her on her cheek (daily). He treated her as his little princess; they were best friends and, for my father, chivalry was not dead. In his efforts to take care of his family, and to have enough money that my Mom would not have to work, he worked two to three jobs, which would require him to be gone twelve to sixteen hours a day. Dad had a sixth grade education, so he worked construction jobs, as an auto mechanic and, at times, would do housekeeping jobs to make ends meet; none of which included medical insurance. He made every effort to give Mom, and all three of his children, everything we needed and most of what we wanted. Mom was Dad's angel, and he loved her dearly. Unfortunately, without health insurance, Mom didn't always get the best medical care and, as a result, was not offered diagnostic tests that would have perhaps diagnosed her illness(s) at early onset.

Not knowing what we didn't know; Dad with a sixth grade education, Mom who must have been petrified of the uncertainty, and me, a teenager who was literally watching my mom fight a downhill battle; we were all lost. We didn't know what to ask for, and when we did ask, we got no answers. I was my mom's biggest advocate. I questioned the doctors; I reminded her of her appointments and made sure she took her medicine; and I researched relentlessly to find a meaning behind what was going on with my mom's medical condition. It had now become a reality; it was an unspoken role  reversal, one in which I embraced, but I had no idea how I would meet the task. At seventeen years old, I was now the primary caregiver for my mom.

Chapter 7

The Eye of the Sparrow...

s I finished high school, I was accepted to more than six major colleges and universities, some of which were out of state. I received several scholarships, but I knew that with my mom's illness advancing, and still not being properly diagnosed, I knew I would need to choose a college/university close to home. In doing so, I could be close enough to get to Mom when or if she needed me. So off to college I went, less than an hour away from home. I immersed myself in my studies, coming home every weekend to check on my mom and to support my dad. I'd often drive back home in the middle of the week as well, in order to accompany my mom to her doctors' appointments. I knew I needed to graduate; again failure was not an option. I was facing a life of responsibilities, not knowing what that fully entailed, but I knew it had only just begun.

Looking into the eyes of my mother, I could often see a woman whose hopes and dreams were now a distant memory. Her empty nest was now truly empty, with all three of her children no longer in the home. I imagined how lonely Mom must have been as my dad continued to work twelve to sixteen hours a day; now not so much to make ends meet, but to pay off medical bills and piling debt from hospital stays and medical procedures for my mom. Mom spent countless hours at home, alone, in bed and often in pain. Still, there were no answers and no definitive diagnosis. Although she expressed her frustration with not knowing what was wrong with her, she was always grateful to God for what she did have. She never complained, never left to go be wild or free; she never binged; she never drank her sorrows or pain away. She just stood still, patient and quiet, waiting on the Lord.

Mom often quoted a Bible verse that resonates in my memory each time I even contemplate complaining.

Matthew 6:26, KJV

Behold the fowls of the air: for they sow not, nether do they reap; nor gather into barns; yet your heavenly Father feedeth them. Are ye not much better than they?

Mom continued to pray Psalm 23, and seek refuge in silence, meditation and prayer. Even after I had graduated college and gotten married (and divorced), I remained close to home: never moving more than two to three hours away so that I could get to her when/if she needed me. I kept my own pain, trials and life situations to myself in order to "spare" my mom (and dad) the burden of worrying about me. They had enough to worry about that they didn't need to concern themselves with my problems. Never asking for money, never coming back home (even after the nasty divorce) and never being a burden to them, I wanted them (especially Mom) to know she could lean and depend on me. She had suffered and sacrificed long enough; she needed peace.

Psalm 23 (KJV)

The Lord is my shepherd; I shall not want.

He maketh me to lie down in green pastures: he lea-deth me beside the still waters.

He restoreth my soul: he leadeth me in the paths of righteousness for his name's sake.

41

Yea, though I walk through the valley of the shadow of death, I will fear no evil: for thou art with me; thy rod and thy staff they comfort me.

Thou preparest a table before me in the presence of mine enemies: thou anointest my head with oil; my cup runneth over.

Surely goodness and mercy shall follow me all the days of my life: and I will dwell in the house of the Lord forever.

Chapter 8

I'm still here...

Mom knew that her current state was not her final status. She had faith that one day she would no longer hurt, no longer be misunderstood, no longer be suffering and would no longer be in pain. Although her faith was strong, she physically began to grow weak. I finished my master's degree, then my doctorate degree: I made many accomplishments personally and professionally. I wanted my parents to be proud. I adored my mom, and wanted to show her she had instilled in me the skills necessary for me to be successful. I took every opportunity to thank Mom for just being my mother: seeing her happy brought me joy. She was a simple woman who only wanted to raise her family and for them to have successful lives.

Although Mom's health was failing, she was still very much alive. She often spoke of her younger days and the fact that earlier in her life, she wanted a career. She said that having her children was her biggest accomplishment: she spoke of missing her two oldest children and her grandchildren. She encouraged me to live my life, but often cautioned me to take care of myself. She only wanted the best for her family; it seemed that her words began to be fewer and fewer. After suffering from constant pain and fatigue for over twenty years, she was finally diagnosed with Parkinson's disease in 1999. She was treated with heavy medications to address the disease, but from 1999 to 2004, she saw numerous doctors and had numerous tests, as she would never feel "normal" on the medications. After seeing numerous doctors, and they all encouraged her to stay on the medications, Mom began to have even more difficulty walking and, at times, even had difficulty speaking, as she would state "the words just won't come out".

Graciously fighting for her life, the tremors suddenly stopped; but on a spring day in 2004, Mom went completely comatose. I had called Mom that morning, like I did every morning on my way to work, but she didn't answer. I lived about two hours away, and had already decided I was going to drive to her if she didn't answer the phone within the hour. Dad then called me to tell me that he had called Mom and, again, she didn't answer the phone.

Dad drove to the house and kept me on the phone. When he walked in the house, he found Mom had somehow rolled out of bed and fallen between the bed and the nightstand. She could not move, could not speak, and stared at the ceiling. He picked her up and placed her on the bed, kept calling her name until her eyes finally started to move. Then she spoke to him, while I listened on the other end of the phone. She said, "I'm dying. I don't have Parkinson's disease. Something is not right." I was already on the way to the house, and arrived shortly thereafter. When I walked in, I knew my mom would never be the same. We took her to the hospital immediately.

Chapter 9

What Mom took....

I was thirty years old and for the last twenty years of my life, I had been caring for my mom. We had been fighting to find her true diagnosis, but to no avail. She had fought her entire life to be normal; to fit in, to be okay. She was beautiful inside and out, but she didn't feel that way. Something happened to her as a child that caused her to turn inward, not talk and rarely open up. Throughout her adult life, she felt second best to other mothers who had careers, who spoke more eloquently, who had college degrees or who had husbands that were successful. She was shy and insecure, so she felt uncomfortable speaking up, even in church. She even felt inferior for not meeting the expectations of her oldest daughter, my only sister. Mom wasn't perfect, but she did the best she could. In her eyes and from the way in which my sister treated her and responded to her, Mom said she felt as if she was never good enough. She said she felt that my sister hated her and was resentful that she was born to a woman of my mom's caliber. I imagined how hurtful it must be to give birth to a child, raise the child the best you can, only to be made to feel inferior or, worse, hated for trying to do her best. In fact, Mom only had a few accomplishments, one of which was having and raising her children. Unfortunately, my sister robbed her of this accomplishment.

Proverbs 20:20, KJV

*Whoso curseth his father or his mother, his lamp
shall be put out in obscure darkness.*

After being rushed to the hospital in 2004, the doctors questioned the diagnosis of Parkinson's disease. Mom remained in the hospital for over a week, having numerous blood tests and scans done. Finally the doctors called all of the family in, my sister of which was the only one that was not there. They advised my dad, my brother and myself that Mom never had Parkinson's disease, and in fact had been treated for several years for something she did not have. We were informed that Mom had multiple sclerosis and, in fact, it was estimated that she had, had it for over twenty years. We were advised that Mom probably only had six months to a year to live, and to take her home and make her comfortable. We were to expect that her disease would progress rapidly, that she probably would lose use of her legs altogether, and that her organs would slowly shut down. I felt as if someone had knocked the wind out of me, but this wasn't about me. I stopped crying and realized that if I felt like this, I could only imagine how Mom felt. My dad was now 69 years old and had one year left until he would retire. Mom was the love of his life, and the doctors had just given her an estimated time of death: her prognosis was not good. She had been fighting her whole life; trying to fit in; trying to care for her children, be a good mother, a good wife, and to simply be normal. She had been from doctor to doctor, had taken one medication after another, had argued and questioned her Parkinson's disease's original diagnosis and had been diagnosed as depressed; only for this moment to finally reveal she, in fact, had been medically (not mentally) ill for over twenty years with multiple sclerosis. She had dealt with not feeling good physically, having had her self-esteem damaged from a very young age, feeling inferior as a parent to her oldest daughter; and now being given her death sentence and told that she only had about six months to live.

In hearing this, I could only imagine how my mother felt. I, myself, felt overwhelmed, as I had sacrificed and dedicated most of my life to ensuring the well-being of my parents. I couldn't help but to look back over my life, my mom's life, my dad's life; our lives, and things just seemed to always be so difficult.

Chapter 10

Why me?

*I*n adversity, it is often the first thing we ask; why me? In retrospect, it is perhaps the easiest thing to do is to have pity for oneself and that is exactly what I started doing. In my mid-30s, divorced, childless and overeducated, I found myself coping with the inevitable loss of my mother, as well as the fact that my young life had already passed me by. I had made a conscious choice to be the primary caregiver for my mom and, if given the opportunity to do it again, I wouldn't change a thing. In spite of this reality, I couldn't deny the other reality of knowing that my social/personal life had somewhat been affected by my decision to remain local, to not have children and to minimize my social interactions, as my time and availability was extremely limited. It was the choice I made, and I faced the consequences thereof.

So, with my mom being given the prognosis of six months to live, I resigned from my jobs, broke my rental agreement on my apartment, sold my furniture and relocated back to my childhood home to care for my mom on a full-time basis. I did what came naturally; I stepped up to the plate to care for my mother. In doing so, it was obvious that I would need financial assistance. It was suggested that because I was not married and didn't have children, it was a given that I would be the best candidate to care full time for our mother. I didn't need convincing; I welcomed the opportunity. Mom deserved only the best. She cared for me when I couldn't care for myself; the least I could do was to return the favor.

It was agreed upon by both my only brother and only sister that this was the right thing to do. None of us wanted Mom to be placed in an assisted living facility, and it was obvious that Dad could not afford to hire a full time-nurse to care for her. Both my brother and sister agreed that they would financially assist me for the one year I cared for our mother. After all, financially assisting me would be less than it would cost to place my mom in an assisted living facility, and less than it would cost to hire a private nurse to care for her full time. This also would allow my dad to continue to work for one year to retirement, as he had planned. It was agreed upon that I, the youngest of the three children and without any children of my own, would take on this responsibility because "it only made sense" and it was the right thing to do.

Here I was in my mid-30s, and I found myself sleeping back in my childhood bedroom; same portraits on the walls, same furnishings in the home and the same memories. I was a grown woman, but felt as if I was once again ten years old; the same age I was when I initially became my mother's primary caregiver. I felt the rush of emotions take over me, almost on a daily basis. Without a job, without a means to care for myself financially, I felt overwhelmed. I felt very vulnerable, as I had no one to fully share my feelings with. All of my closest friends were working, had full-time jobs and careers, or they were traveling with their families and living their lives. I didn't know anyone my age that was caring for their elderly parents. I wasn't even forty years old yet, and I quite honestly felt as if my life was ending. I was overwhelmed and, at times, felt alone. I found solace in reading the Bible and meditating. I found out who my closest friends and loved ones were during this time, as many family and friends were nowhere to be found. I needed support in every way imaginable. Unmarried, childless, and now my best friend was dying right before my eyes; nevertheless, I had to be strong because I had no other choice. I had to be strong because my mom needed me. I kept telling myself, "Sheila, you can do this; it's only a year": it's the least I could do for the woman that had sacrificed so much for me, for all of us.

From day to day, week to week, my mom's medical condition declined. She went from walking with a cane, to walking with a walker, to not walking at all. Within three months, she lost muscle strength in her legs and her internal organs began to shut down. She became incontinent; so I washed her hair, I picked her up and placed her in the bathtub, I bathed her, clothed her and I fed her. She knew she was dying, and this thing they called multiple sclerosis was taking over. On some days she cried; on other days I cried; on most days, we cried together. It was inevitable; the thing we feared most had become a reality. Death would soon be upon her. I wasn't ready to lose my mom; she was my best friend. I could tell this woman anything and she would never judge me. She'd look at me, after I had done something foolish, and just stare, and without calling me stupid or immature. I knew what she was saying. Even when she tried to be mean I saw right through her. She was so innocent, so afraid; she'd often put on a "mean" face to appear as if she was tough when, underneath, she was that ten-year-old,

scared little girl. She was the little girl that had once been wronged as a child. I couldn't help but see her innocence each time I looked in her eyes; she cried for help. I've been told that the eyes are the windows to the soul. In her eyes I saw heaven, a place that would eventually embrace her.

Chapter 11

The forgotten promise...

After caring for my mom on a full-time basis for six months, I hadn't received any financial assistance from my brother. He had promised to help me financially, and so had my sister. In the first six months of me caring for our mother, I had received a total of about $300 from my sister and nothing from my brother. They both promised they would assist me by sending me at least $500-$600 a month, and in doing so, they gave me reassurance that I would at least have enough money to cover my basic needs. I trusted them, but when they fell through, it added to my feelings of despair.

As a result of not receiving the financial assistance agreed upon from my brother, I resorted to making ends meet any way I could (other than illegal or immoral acts). I had been living off my credit cards and draining my savings account in order to just get by. I needed food and toiletries. I still had expenses, as I was in my mid-30s, a grown woman with a master's degree and over twelve years of successful professional experience. Did my siblings forget their promise? After all, this was not just my mom; this was "our" mom I was caring for. Both of my siblings were active in the military, for over twenty years, married and had made the promise to me that they would assist me. They left me hanging and holding a major responsibility. Without having any previous history of asking for assistance from them, and never receiving any money from either of them, I had no reason to believe they would not make good on their promises to me. I trusted them, I loved them and I looked up to them. They were my siblings, and I had no reason not to believe them. I was unfortunately mistaken.

It was the fall of 2004, approximately six months after her diagnosis and the time in which I started caring for her full-time; her physical health had drastically declined. Her arms and fingers began to contract, and she lost use of both hands and all fingers. She was now completely bedridden. Her nurses and doctors could not believe she was still living, in spite of her physical condition. Her mental capacity was still intact, but her body was beginning to shut down. Mom occasionally talked about the presidency, current events and things that happened ten years earlier, and she even spoke of when she was a teenager. I was amazed that her mental capacity had not failed. She was still very much Mom, still able to organize and plan accordingly, but she physically couldn't care for herself at all. In fact, Mom and Dad wanted to make sure that things were appropriately taken care of; it was at this time they completely planned their funerals, updated their wills and made all arrangements, down to the color and design of their caskets. However morbid it may have seemed to me at the time, I would later (eight years later) appreciate them making their final wishes known.

Here I was, struggling to eat: in fact, I had resorted to eating beans from a can and Vienna sausages, as I had no money. My savings had run out and my credit cards were to their limits. I felt so alone and desolate. Because I could not afford to go to the beauty salon, my hair had fallen out, and I developed adult acne from the stress. I started experiencing stomach pains and body aches, and my once joyful demeanor had become very flat: I had no money and no one to turn to. When I finally spoke to my sister about the money she had promised to give me, she explained that the $50-$100 she was giving me here and there was all she could afford. It wasn't much, but it was better than nothing. On the other hand, my brother hadn't given me anything for six months. When I spoke with him about it, he told me he couldn't make good on his promise, because he had spoken too soon when he promised to assist me. He told me that he was saving his money to buy his daughter a car, which he ultimately didn't buy her. Wow, how could they do this to me? This was *our* mother I was caring for: cooking, cleaning, lifting, changing, repositioning, bathing and washing twenty-four/seven without relief, this was what I did. The physical, emotional and psychological demands were exponential; while I simultaneously pretended to be strong as I watched my father strongly deal with the inevitable loss of his soul mate, his best friend, the mother of his children, his wife. Didn't my siblings or anyone, for that matter, realize that I needed help, that I was alone, broke and depressed? Better yet, didn't anyone care?

"MY MOTHER GETS DRESSED"

It is impossible for my mother to do even the simplest things

for herself anymore

so we do it together, get her dressed. I choose the clothes

without zippers or buckles or straps,

clothes that are simple but elegant, and easy to get into.

Otherwise, it's just like every other day. After bathing, getting

dressed. The stockings go on first.

This time, it's the new ones, the special ones with opaque

black triangles

that she's never worn before, bought just two weeks ago

at her favorite department store.

We start with the heavy, careful stuff of the right toes

into the stocking tip then a smooth yank past the knob of

her ankle

and over her cool, smooth calf then the other toe

cool ankle, smooth calf up the legs and the pantyhose is

coaxed to her waist.

You're doing great, Mom, I tell her as we ease her body against

mine, rest her whole weight against me to slide her black dress

with the black empire collar

over her head struggle her fingers through the dark tunnel of

the sleeve.

I reach from the outside deep into the dark for her hand,

grasp where I can't see for her touch. *You've got to help me a*
little here, Mom
I tell her then her fingertips touch mine and we work her fingers through the sleeve's mouth
together, then we rest, her weight against me before threading
the other fingers, wrist, forearm, elbow, bicep and now over
the head....

An excerpt from Daphne Gottlieb, *Final Girl*

My dad was still struggling to pay medical bills and to pay for
all of the medical equipment and medications my mom needed.
Mom lived past the six months the doctors had anticipated she
would live. We were moving into a full year past the day she
was giving the prognosis, and Dad and I were still keeping our
promise, in spite of what others had failed to do. At sixty-nine
years old, Dad was still working and his body had become frail.
I couldn't, and wouldn't dare, ask him for money, when I felt
it was not his responsibility to care for me. I was depressed in
mind, body and soul. I was embarrassed to let anyone see me in
the state that I was in, so I ignored phone calls from my friends or
invitations for anyone who wanted to come visit me. Although I
wanted support, needed to confide in someone about what I was
going through, I kept everything on a surface level, dealing with
it all on my own and praying to God for comfort and resolution.

I had no reservations about sacrificing my well-being to care for my mom; after all, she was in her final days and she cared for me when I couldn't care for myself. I was grateful that I had the opportunity to care for my mom and at the one-year mark, Dad retired. I moved out and went back to work (three jobs), in order to dig myself out of the hole I was in, in every aspect of the word.

Chapter 12

Peace be still....

After Dad retired at seventy years old, and I had relocated and went back to work, he became suddenly ill and was diagnosed with leukemia.

Mark 4:39 KJV

And he arose, and rebuked the wind, and said unto the sea, Peace, be still. And the wind ceased, and there was a great calm.

Lord, you know....

From 2005 to 2011, I had a personal struggle. I struggled to finally regain a healthy state mentally, physically and financially. Although I embraced and stepped up to the opportunity to care for my Mom, I experienced some very serious obstacles along the way. After being left out to dry by my siblings, while caring for my mom full-time for an entire year, I depleted all of my savings, ran up my balance on my credit cards, sold my furniture and my car, broke my lease and quit my jobs. I struggled to get back to where I was financially, emotionally and spiritually prior to taking on the responsibility of caring for both my Mom (and my Dad). It took me six years to get back on track. I worked two to three jobs simultaneously; I rebuilt my credit, bought a house, finished my PhD, paid off debt and started my own consulting company. I traveled to several different countries, and regained communication with close friends and relatives. Although I forgave my siblings for leaving me to care for our mother, without the support they promised and for putting me in a financial state of disaster, I didn't forget what they had done to me. This is something I still personally struggle with to this day. The devastation of what they did to me was in fact probably the worst thing that anyone has done to me in my life. Needless to say, I moved on as I had no choice. Now it was time to focus on caring for Mom (and Dad) even more.

Mom had lived seven years past the prognosis of having six months to live. Dad had lived six years past the three-month prognosis he had been given to live. This, in fact, proved to me that no man knows our date of expiration, only God. At this point in my life, I made a promise to live my life to the fullest; to have no regrets and make no apologies for doing what's right! I made a promise to hold my head high, to love and adore Mom and Dad, just as I had always done. It was Mom's dying wish to remain at home and to be with her husband when she passed. For this reason, every effort was made to make the home as comfortable as possible.

It was 2010, right about the time Mom was placed on hospice and stated to be "actively dying", my sister, the only one I have, was going through a divorce and decided to move into our parents' home to "help care for them" in their last days. This is the same sister that Mom said resented her, the same person that rarely came home to visit, and the same one that stiffed me on her financial promise when I cared for our mom full-time for a full year. We had hopes that perhaps in our parents' final days, my sister would step up and amend any discourse or ill feelings she had towards them. Although I was skeptical, as I've always felt that it's difficult for a person to change their true self, I prayed for the best and warned my parents to think hard about allowing her to move back into the home. My parents had hearts of gold and seeing their oldest daughter going through her second divorce, soon to be a single mom of four children, their hearts broke for her, and they believed she had well intentions.

Luke 14:26 KJV

If any [man] come to me, and hate not his father, and mother, and wife, and children, and brethren, and sisters, yea, and his own life also, he cannot be my disciple.

Chapter 13
Don't be disillusioned...

Shortly after my sister arrived and moved in with her three youngest children, she quickly stopped cooking, stopped buying any groceries and made an open statement to Mom, Dad, myself and my brother...

I'm here to help, but I'm not changing any diapers and I'm not lifting Mom!

My mom had always told me, "Baby, don't be disillusioned; a leopard never changes his spots." She told me she was at times "scared" of my sister, and that she felt my sister hated her for being her mother. I felt helpless; as both my mom and dad could not believe she had moved back into the home to simply ignore their household rules and blatantly use them to live rent-free. She failed to change my mom's diapers, failed to wash her hair or even bring her a glass of water. Most days, my sister and her children would walk by my mom's hospital bed and not even say hello. After being so overwhelmed with emotions, I offered to my parents to physically remove my sister from the home, but it was their wish that she be left alone. I lay next to my mom countless days and nights on end, watching her sleep, watching the sheet move up and down as she breathed. I listened to her oxygen machine inhale, then exhale. I touched her face, kissed her cheeks and let her know how much I loved and adored her. I told her how much it crushed my heart to see her suffering, to know that she was afraid of my sister, and I empathized with how she must have felt. Bedridden and facing the inevitable, Mom had fought a long fight: she, in fact, had defeated all odds. Although my father was fighting cancer, he was still mobile, still able to drive and still able to cook for himself. He was becoming weaker as the days passed, but he was adamant that his oldest daughter and her three youngest children be left to remain in the home, in spite of her blatant disrespect for his rules. He loved them; Mom did too, regardless of the way in which they were being treated. They were God-fearing parents, and they believed that what a man sows that he shall also reap.

Leviticus 20:9, KJV –

For every one that curseth his father or his mother shall be surely put to death: he hath cursed his father or his mother; his blood [shall be] upon him.

Dad called a family meeting and read off the contents of his will. Although we already knew the specifics of the will ever since 2004, when Mom and Dad wrote it, Dad decided in 2011 it was time to reiterate the specifics of their will again. He advised my sister that he was unhappy with the fact that she had not held up to her promise to help them, but because she was their oldest child, and because she had three teenage children, they would allow her to live in the home until she could find another place to live. Dad told her that he was saddened and disappointed in the way in which she had treated Mom all her life, especially now that Mom was literally on her deathbed. Dad was still very much in love with Mom, and just as I did, he often put his needs aside in order to make sure Mom had what she needed. How could he not, as Mom was as delicate as a flower and very humble and unselfish, even in her last days. He was disappointed in my sister and hurt by the way in which she obviously used their illnesses to use them, by living in their home rent-free and choosing to not assist them in any way, financially or otherwise. Although Mom and Dad kept their wills the same, they made it known that they

69

would leave me as the executor of their estate, as they were not happy about the way in which my sister was treating them.

As Mom stated, I kept in mind that I should not be disillusioned; my sister was a wolf in sheep's clothing. She'd greet you with a kiss, while simultaneously stabbing you in the back. I'm not exactly sure what happened to her, or where it all went wrong, but what I do know is it was deliberate for her to move back into Mom's home, when it was clearly apparent she resented her from a very young age. In fact, Mom said she resented her since she was a little girl. I confronted my sister, and so did my brother, as watching her mistreat our parents was unbearable. She adamantly denied misusing her position, or that she was doing anything wrong. It was the *poor me* card she pulled out each time. "Poor me. I'm a two- time divorcee; poor me, I'm single and I have four children; poor me this, poor me that." Regardless of the cards we've been dealt, it doesn't give us the right to take advantage of the next person, especially not our dying parents. Her actions were inexcusable, but all the more reason for me to love and adore my parents even more.

Had I not promised both my mom and dad that I would not address my sister, that I would not physically remove her from my parents' home and that I would not even argue with her, I would not be writing this book. I perhaps would be behind bars, as I despised her for the way in which she treated them. She was mean, and my parents were at times afraid of her. Perhaps she was dealing with mental demons that had taken over her mind, as she was clearly not a rational and loving person. In fact, I always felt uncomfortable being around her. My parents were clearly stressed when they were in her presence: they felt indebted to her and her children. Although she did not physically abuse them, she mentally and emotionally tortured them. To me, what was very apparent was that my sister was a woman who clearly hated her parents, who had been resentful to her own mother, and very verbal about her dislike and hatred towards me for loving and adoring our mother (and father). She was evil in every sense of the word and could not be trusted. I had no one to turn to who would believe me, or even entertain my thoughts. Regardless of my sister's issues and hateful ways, I did not allow her to get in the way of me loving and caring for my mom. So, for the next year and a half, I stayed visible, present and active, even more than I had been for the past thirty-plus years for my parents.

Chapter 14

It is well....

Matthew 15:4-6, KJV

For God commanded, saying, Honour thy father and mother:
and, He that curseth father or mother, let him die the death.
But ye say, Whosoever shall say to [his] father or [his] mother,
[It is] a gift, by whatsoever thou mightest be profited by me;
And honour not his father or his mother, [he shall be free].
Thus have ye made the commandment of God of none effect
by your tradition.

y mom was the apple of my eye; I adored her and she adored me. I continued to send her flowers, change her diapers, kiss her cheeks, and tell her how beautiful and special she was to me. I told her how much I loved her, how much she meant to me. She told me she was happy with the woman I had become; she reassured me that she was proud of me, that she loved me and that she was thankful for all that I had done for her. She thanked me for respecting her wishes to leave my sister alone and to let God handle her. She told me that there was nothing I could do to my sister that would be worse than what would become of her. She told me to let her be and to let God take care of the situation. She told me she knew she didn't have long and that I would need to be strong. She told me that I would soon be in this world without a mother, and she reminded me that to be absent in the body is to be present with the Lord.

The week before the angels took my mother home, I was in the bathroom applying my makeup and combing my hair. I saw my mother looking at me out of the corner of her eye. She couldn't move, but she was watching me. As I saw her looking at me, I turned to her and asked, "Mom, are you okay, do you need anything?" She said to me, "No, you're beautiful." I leaned down to kiss her cheek and to remind her that I looked just like her. For what she saw in me was exactly the same as what I saw in her. I told her she was beautiful, and I thanked God she was my mother.

Little did I know that, that would be the last conversation she and I would have. Seven days later, around 2 a.m. on Sunday morning, I was awakened out of my sleep as I heard my mother's voice say Sheila. Although I was over fifty miles away, I heard her call my name and I knew she was gone. I sat with my phone in my hand, as I waited for the phone to ring. When it rang thirty minutes later, the voice on the other end was my brother's saying, "She's gone". The funeral arrangements were all on me: as my sister sat back and watched me plan it all, while I simultaneously had to be strong for my dad. At my mother's second funeral and burial, my sister did not attend. Although I could not understand it, this was validation to me; that she felt no sense of connection for our mother. She, in fact, hated my mom, and it was now clearly apparent. Her only excuse for not attending the funeral and burial was that she "had other things to do". I couldn't understand it then, and I don't understand it now. In fact, I don't think I ever will. Now that Mom has passed, she no longer has to feel second best or not good enough. She is finally at peace, as she had suffered long enough. In fact, she lived eight years past the time in which the doctors believed she would live.

Mom was exceptional: she fought her entire life, and never complained. She was the strongest woman I've ever known. She remained immobile and in constant pain, unable to even scratch her own face for eight long years, yet she never complained. To be in the presence of a woman as strong as she, I am blessed. I am blessed to have even known her. I am blessed to have shared forty-plus years of my life with her. I'm blessed to have the same blood as she: I am blessed to have been raised and loved by her. I am blessed to be her daughter, for she was a rare jewel; none other was like her, none others to be like her.

I have no regrets for the things I did for my mom, or the sacrifices I made to make her time here as comfortable as possible. She was an angel given to me for only a short period of time. Although she spent most of her life in emotional and physical pain, she knew she was loved. She found comfort in knowing she would once again be with the Lord, and she would no longer be in pain. She knew that there wasn't anything I wouldn't do for her. It's been almost two years since she's been gone, and I miss her just as if it was yesterday that she passed away. For the first year, it was very difficult for me to even breathe. Although I've been able to cope, it has been a daily challenge. To live life without the one person who would not judge me and who loved me unconditionally is, at times, unbearable. Writing this book has been instrumental in my healing. My mother's story needed to be told; her voice was never heard. Through this book, it is my goal to be her voice and to tell her story. She was a beautiful woman, both inside and out.

This is not only the story of my mother, but this is the story of a very integral piece of my life. For my mother and I had a connection, as many mothers and daughters share a bond that is unbreakable. It has always been my motto to live life to the fullest, no regrets and with no reservations. I've written this book to tell not only my mother's story, but the story of many mothers and the bond they share with their daughters, as my mother was my best friend. Although my life will never be the same, I still feel her presence on a daily basis: the life she lived will forever live on in me. It is well, Mom; I miss you and I love you.

2 Corinthians 5:8, KJV

We are confident, I say, and willing rather to be absent from the body, and to be present with the Lord.